Wow!
Your Body

A Book of Extraordinary Facts

First published 2018
This edition published 2019 by Kingfisher
an imprint of Macmillan Children's Books
6 Briset Street, London, EC1M 5NR
Associated companies throughout the world
www.panmacmillan.com

Author: Jacqueline McCann and Emma Dods
Design and styling: Liz Adcock
Cover design: Liz Adcock
Illustrations: Marc Aspinall & Ste Johnson

ISBN: 978-0-7534-4533-4

Copyright © Macmillan Publishers International Ltd 2013, 2018, 2019

Illustrations in this book previously appeared in *Wow! Human Body*,
published by Kingfisher in 2013.

9 8 7 6 5 4 3 2 1
1TR/0819/UNTD/WKT/140WFO

A CIP catalogue record for this book is available from the British Library.

Printed in China

Wow! Your Body

A Book of Extraordinary Facts

KINGFISHER

What are we?

Human beings come in all shapes and sizes, but mostly, we're all the same.

On the outside, people look quite different to one another. We may have different coloured skin, eyes and hair ...

... but we all have a body, a head, legs and arms. And on the inside, we have a brain, a heart and lots of other organs that help our body work.

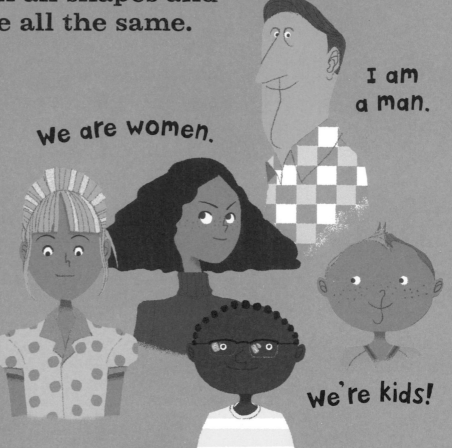

We are women.

I am a man.

we're kids!

My dark skin **protects** me from the sun!

Some people have dark skin. Some people have white skin. Most people have skin that is a shade of brown.

4

We're cells. We may be tiny ...

... but we're **very important!**

I'm a nerve cell.

Wow!
Your body is mostly made of water. You also have 37,000,000,000,000 cells in your body! That's 37 trillion!

Cells are the building blocks of all living things. You have roughly 200 different kinds of cell and everything that happens in your body, is because of them!

I'm a **red blood** cell.

Your cells work together all the time to build organs, such as your brain and your heart. They protect your body, too, and help to fight off disease and illness.

We're super-strong **muscle cells!**

I'm a **white blood** cell.

Growing up

We all start life as a bunch of cells. Gradually, we grow from baby to child and then to grown-up!

You start life as tiny **cells!**

Children grow quickly and learn to become more independent. They are often very lively. Are you?

gurgle

When you are a baby, you have a big head and short legs, but you grow very fast! A baby needs lots of love!

You **grow** fastest in spring and summer!

Getting bigger

When you are a newborn baby, you need an adult to feed you and look after you. As you grow, you become more independent and need adults less and less.

When you are a teenager, your body starts to change - a lot!

By the time you reach 18 years of age, you are an adult and your body has done most of its growing!

When you are 45, your body starts to slow down. You don't have as much energy as you did before. Oh dear!

Not so fast, kiddo!

Go grey

Your body might stop growing when you're an adult ... but your nose and ears don't! They get bigger and bigger! Your bones aren't as strong as they once were, and your hair will probably turn grey.

What big ears you've got, Dear!

Big bones, little bones

What holds you up? Your bones, of course! If you didn't have them, you'd be like a wobbly jelly.

is it humerus?

want to hear a joke?

Your bones are the scaffolding that holds you together! Altogether, your bones make up your skeleton. It protects the organs inside your body and helps you move!

Your smallest bone is inside your ear. It's the size of a grain of rice.

...At the bottom of your spine (in your bottom) are four tiny bones joined together, like a mini tail!

i've got a tail, too!

Your spine is a chain of bones running down your back. Your spine and leg bones help you to stand and walk.

The strongest and longest bone in your body is in your leg – it's called the femur.

you have **52 bones** in your two feet.

When you're a baby, you have 300 to 350 bones. As you grow, small bones in your body stick, or fuse, together. By the time you're a grown-up you'll have 206 bones.

WOW!

Your skull is like a hard hat protecting your brain. It's made of 22 bones that stick together as you grow. Your teeth are part of your skeleton, too!

Muscle power

More than half your body is made of muscles. Their main job is to get your body moving!

Muscles support your skeleton and keep your shape. They help you walk, jump, run and win races!

MOVE OVER, we're coming through!

I'm the fastest. I've got four legs!

When you start to run, your brain sends a message to your muscles and bones to get going! Your muscles work in pairs with your bones, stretching and relaxing.

Wow!

There are more than 650 named muscles in the human body. Did you know that you use 300 of them just to stand?

Did you know that your muscles have memory? The more you practise something, the better your muscles become at remembering, which is important when you learn a new sport.

FINISH

oh my gluteus!

ouch!

What happens when you fall over? You are saved by your bottom, otherwise known as your gluteus (say gloot-y-us) maximus, the largest muscle in your body!

You use 17 muscles when you smile!

Heart and blood

Blood is the red liquid that fuels your body. Your heart does the hard work pumping it around your body.

Pump it up

Your heart is an organ made of two super strong muscles working together like pumps. It squeezes blood around your body, then relaxes, before squeezing again.

Blood is super stuff! It has tiny cells which carry everything your body needs to help you breathe, keep you warm, fight off diseases, think and grow!

Blood vessels and arteries are like roads and motorways, carrying blood around your body.

Red blood cells carry oxygen.

Wow!

Without you even knowing, your heart works very hard. It beats about 90 times a minute. It will beat about three billion times in your lifetime!

White blood cells fight disease!

Big heart

Your heart grows as you grow. You can't see your heart, but it sits behind your ribs, slightly on the left-hand side.

It's important to keep your heart healthy! The best way to do this is to do lots of exercise, eat fruit and vegetables and drink lots of water!

Let's hop, skip and jump ...

Your heart, blood and arteries work together to carry vitamins around your body and keep you in good working order. They also carry away any chemicals your body doesn't need.

Control centre

Your brain is more clever and powerful than the world's most powerful computer!

Your brain collects messages from your body and the world around you. It stores all the information it receives for you to use when you need it.

I'm brainy...

This bit is good at reading and knowing left from right.

The front part of your brain works out language and maths.

The back of your brain recognizes colour.

LEFT RIGHT   6 + 5 = 11

HELLO

GOODBYE!

This part controls movement.

skip!

skip, don't trip!

Messages flow from your brain, through the brain stem and down to the rest of your body.

This area of your brain helps you to understand language and music.

14

... but an elephant's brain is **bigger!**

Wow!

An elephant has the biggest brain of any animal on land. Its brain is four times bigger than an adult human's.

Chimpanzees are clever, too. They use tools to do jobs (like us) and they are almost unbeatable at some computer games!

Any more bananas?

Rats and mice are quick learners and they're good at puzzles!

I'm clever, too.

Skin and hair

Skin wraps around your skeleton and muscles, keeping it all together. What else does it do?

Your skin is a bit like a waterproof coat; it keeps the rain and the germs out. It stops all your blood and gooey bits from leaking out, too!

Wow!

The surface of your skin is constantly rubbing off in tiny flakes as new skin is made underneath. The dust in your house is mostly made of those tiny flakes!

Hi, I'm a mighty dust mite!

Yummy!

Teeny tiny creatures called dust mites live in your house, munching on dead flakes of your skin – they're everywhere, but they're too small to see.

You have hair ALL over your body. The only place you don't have it is the palm of your hands, the soles of your feet, and your lips!

The roots of your hair, called follicles, grow from your skin, too. You even have hairs up your nose. They trap dust and nasty germs, so you don't breathe them in.

It's true

Straight hair grows from round follicles. Curly hair grows from oval follicles.

what colour is your hair?

I have hair on my top lip. It's called a moustache.

Red hair is the rarest hair colour in the world.

Blonde-haired people have more hairs on their head than other people.

Everyone loses 50-150 hairs a day. Mine has stopped growing back!

17

Eyes and ears

You have five main senses, which allow you to connect to the world: smell, touch, taste, sight and hearing.

who's a pretty Polly?

Your eyes are on the front of your face, looking forwards. This means you can see in front of you and a bit to the sides, but you can't see behind you.

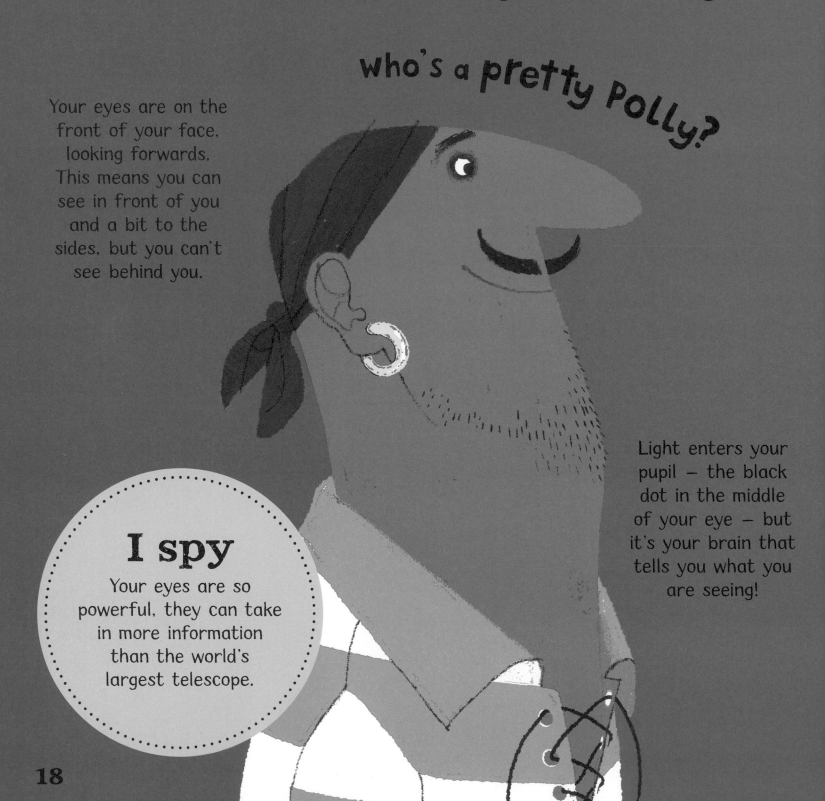

Light enters your pupil – the black dot in the middle of your eye – but it's your brain that tells you what you are seeing!

I spy
Your eyes are so powerful, they can take in more information than the world's largest telescope.

18

I hear you, Captain!

Ear, ear

The outside of your ear is shaped to catch sounds and channel them into your ear. Tiny hairs pick up the vibrations and send messages to your brain.

Animals and birds are often better at seeing and hearing than people are.

squawk!

A macaw is a kind of parrot. It has eyes on either side of its head, which means it can see all around, even behind!

Like all parrots, macaws are very good listeners. They can hear high-pitched sounds that people can't hear.

Wow!

Ears don't just help you to hear, they help you to balance, too. They tell your body that you're lying down at night, or standing up during the day!

Smell, taste, touch

Imagine if you couldn't smell your favourite dinner, or taste a crunchy apple? What if you couldn't touch?

How do you know if something smells stinky, sweet or sour? Clever little cells at the back of your nose send a message to your brain to let you know!

cake feels squidgy ...

Sniff ...

If you didn't have a sense of touch, you wouldn't be able to tell is something is hot, cold, itchy, painful, or very heavy!

As you grow older, you gradually lose your sense of smell and taste.

A baby learns how things feel by putting them into its mouth!

Your sense of smell is connected to your memory too. Freshly cut grass might make you think of a summer picnic. Or, maybe smelly socks make you think of your big brother?

smells yummy ... and tastes delicious!

Wow!

Your nose recognizes more than 10,000 different smells! And it's your sense of smell that actually tells you most about what you are tasting!

The first sense a baby uses when it's born, is smell!

Your tongue is the most sensitive part of your body. It has nearly 5000 taste buds to help you taste different flavours.

Grapes on the loose ...

21

Down it goes

What happens to your lunch after you've smelled, tasted and eaten it? Let's see!

When food is in your mouth, your body starts to break it up into little pieces. First your teeth go to work ...

Open wide. Lunch on its way!

1
Sharp teeth do the cutting.

2
Molar teeth at the back do the crushing.

3
A juice called saliva mixes with your food.

4
Your tongue helps push food to the back of your mouth.

5
The jiggly uvula stops food going the wrong way!

22   Are we lunch?

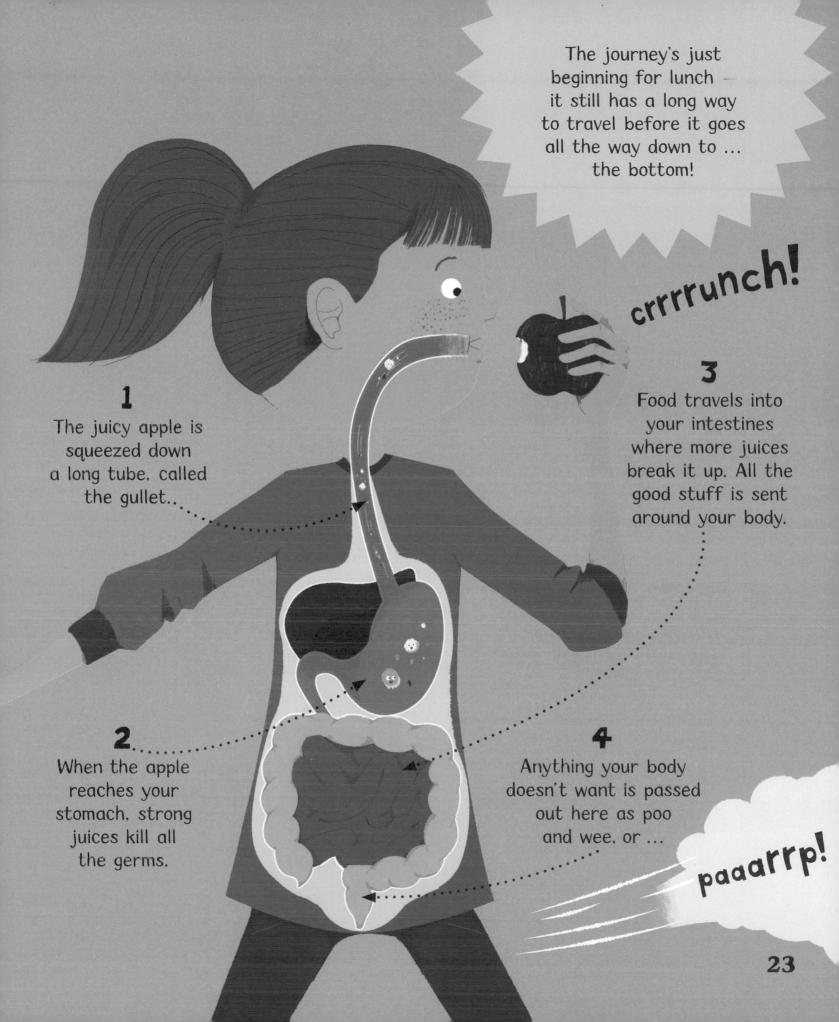

The journey's just beginning for lunch – it still has a long way to travel before it goes all the way down to ... the bottom!

crrrrunch!

1
The juicy apple is squeezed down a long tube, called the gullet..

2
When the apple reaches your stomach, strong juices kill all the germs.

3
Food travels into your intestines where more juices break it up. All the good stuff is sent around your body.

4
Anything your body doesn't want is passed out here as poo and wee, or ...

paaarrp!

23

Windy tummy

Sometimes gas escapes from your body, either through a burp or a fart! Has this ever happened to you?

It takes more than a day for food to go in one end and out the other. Your body pushes out what it doesn't need as poo and wee.

When you eat and drink, you breathe in air which is made of gases. Bacteria in your intestines make gas too. Eventually all those gases need to come out!

Farting and burping is ...

...noisy

paaaarrp!

but **normal!**

You will spend about three years of your life on the toilet. Yeeeew!

Farty food!

Beans, cabbage, artichoke, peas, apples and sprouts all make you fart more. But they are very good for you!

Scientists have spent a long time studying what happens when astronauts fart in space! The farts don't go anywhere — they just hover!

Astronaut suits are fitted with special filters that get rid of poisonous gases!

In Space, no one can hear you...

...fart!

Is it night time?

Night, night

Why is sleeping so important? Does your body do anything when it is tucked up, fast asleep?

It takes most people 7 minutes to fall asleep.

Sleeping helps you to remember things and to learn, which is why you have to go to bed early on a school night! Children need between 10 and 12 hours sleep a night!

While you're sleeping, your body works very hard for you, growing muscles and bones and making itself better.

Zzzzz!

Wow!

You will spend about a third of your life sleeping! So if you live to be 90 years old, that's 30 years of snoozing!

What happens if you don't get enough sleep? Your body doesn't work so well, your reactions are slower and it's more difficult to concentrate. You'll probably be a bit grumpy, too!

Sweet dreams!

Why dream?

No one knows for sure why we dream. Scientists think it might be a good way to sort our memories, or to tidy up your brain after you've had a hard day's work.

Some people do unbelievable things when they're asleep! They go for a walk (that's sleepwalking) or play the piano. Sleepwalkers can even cook or draw amazing pictures.

Shhhhh! More amazing body facts this way . . .

Amazing body

Your body does lots of amazing things, without you telling it to — these are called reflexes.

Tee-he-he! Giggle! Giggle!

tickle tickle!

Ticklish?

It is impossible to tickle yourself because your brain knows what is coming and ignores the "tickle". It only works if someone else does it for you!

You may think you are in control of your body, but it's your reflexes that make you ...

... blink if something touches your eye.

... yawn when you feel sleepy.

... hiccup without knowing why.

... cough and sneeze. Achoo!

... shiver when you're cold ... and sometimes when you're scared!

28

Keep still!

I can't!

Standing on one leg isn't easy! But even to stand on two legs, you have to keep shifting your weight, or you'll fall over!

Time to get moving! Walk this way ...

If you take 8000 to 10,000 steps a day, then in your lifetime, you will have walked the same distance as four times around the world!

Where are we going?

Wow!

Have you you ever noticed the swirly patterns on your fingertips? Those patterns are called fingerprints. No one else has the same patterns as you!

It's true

It isn't only your fingerprints that are unique to you – no one has the same toe prints either! Your lips, earlobes, tongue print and teeth are all unique to you, too!

29

Ancient body facts

Thousands of years ago, the Ancient Egyptians and Romans had some funny ideas about bodies!

The Ancient Egyptians were a clever bunch — they built the pyramids after all! But strange as it seems to us, when cats died, their owners shaved off their eyebrows!

Ancient Egyptian kings, called pharaohs, had people who worked for them as official bottom wipers!

My cat died. NOW I have to shave my eyebrows!

Squeak

Nearly 3000 years ago, in Ancient Egypt, if you had bad breath, the dentist put a hot, dead mouse in your mouth to cure you. Eeeek!